Voice

From

Home

A collection of Poetry

By

Linda Nonyelu

Copyright © 2022.

DEDICATION

Dedicated to God Almighty for his strength and courage to write this work of art

Dedicated to my Father of the blessed memory who had always wanted me to do this, I know he will be proud of me wherever he is.

Dedicated also to my family and friends, who had been my driving force and had contributed in one way or the other to see this book to be a reality.

TABLE OF CONTENTS

Shameless love
My mother's house
Sweet painful memories
The sound of music
Love is to life
Childhood memories
Before you leap,look
Who could have believed?

HAVE YOU SEEN THIS WOMAN?

She is the fragile glass decanter,
That we all behold and admire
She has the wise eyes of mother Teresa,
And the gentle touch that warm our soul,
Like hot milk served by our grandmother on a sleepless night
Her speech modifies her presence
She is not the toy that men play with
She is a table marked " reserved"
She is an exhibit marked "look but don't touch"

Have you seen this woman?
She is the envy of the ordinary,
And the object of the connoisseur
She is the goal of her daughter,
And the gem of her husband
Her words are far more glamorous than her clothes

She is rich, whether she lives in the projects or condominium

Have you seen this woman?
She is covered with jewels of glistening eye and luster of hope

Age cannot rob her,
For she is far more than smooth skin and strong bones
Class is always timeless
She is not the faddish, foolish, fanatical icon of the day
She is timeless as a concerto in C minor.

Have you seen this woman?
She is a moment of treasure to be admired
She is an investment paying dividend to all whom she is
exposed
She is a lady of majesty and elegance
Her riches are beyond counting
She is adorned with diamond in her eyes and rubies in her
smile
She is the jasper stone of riches and the rich onyx of the night.

WHEN A LADY HAS A LOVER

When a lady has a lover
He will be the warm hand touching of her back,
Giving her the stability to go forward
He will give her the feeling of uncompromising love,
As she faces the various ages and stages of life
He gives her body release, her mind a melody,
And her spirit a gust of wind that makes her able to soar like an
eagle

When lady has a lover
Her eyes sparkle, her smile radiates
And her voice is calm and passionate
Her heart is peaceful for she feels secure
And can close her eyes and rest her head on his shoulder

When a lady has a lover
He works the night shift and watches over her in the dark
He is the one who she can talk to,
When her words can't describe what she is feeling
He understands what she says, and what she feels.

A BROKEN WOMAN

Have you ever seen a broken woman?
You cannot tell her by her clothes or hair
Nor can you describe her
 By her race or number of degrees she has obtained from a
university
There is slight traces of scars behind her makeup
A blank, dead stare that neither her eye liner nor shadow can
give life to
You will see a smile that fades too quickly
Or a planed glance that stares into a past too hideous to be
described and too hideous to be forgotten

You will see the empty gaze in the eyes of one who has seen
hellfire,
And been scourged by a story that she has no courage to tell
She often hides her helplessness in anger
She wraps herself in bitterness

The only protection she can muster is her own
She is similar to a tame animal playing Savage
Hoping no one will know her beneath her growl,
 There are no teeth, just tears
There are hot blazing tears that comes out in the night
Like owls and hanged perched on her eyelid

She puts on mask on her face to go to work
She is a vase that has been cracked, leaking life , losing love
Relationships slip through her fingers like sand held too tightly.

HAVE YOU SEEN THE ONE I LOVE?

Have you seen the one I love?
He is dark and dazzling,
His head is finest gold,and his hair is as black as raven
His eyes are like doves set like jewels washed in milk
I lose focus when he looks into my eyes
His cheek are like garden of spices giving off fragrance
His lips are like lilies, dripping with liquid myrrh

Have you seen the one I love?
His arms are like rounded bars of gold
Oh! the peace when he places those arms around me
His body is as bright as ivory
I could see myself through his skin
His legs are like marble pillars, set in socket of finest gold

Have you seen the one I love?
The king of my heart
The crown upon my head
The eyes which I see through
He's better than ten thousand others.

MKPURUMMA (My Beauty)

Mkpurumma m!
Your beauty radiates like the sun
Illuminating light to the nook and cranny of the earth
Your hair is like a flock of goats, descending for the hills of
Gilead
Your eyes are like doves,
Besides springs of living water
Melting the hearts of whoever you look upon

Your nose is as the tower of Lebanon, overlooking Damascus
Your lips are like scarlet ribbon,
Tempting and inviting for a succulent kiss
Your teeth are as white as snow and like flock of sheep they
are like twin
Your neck is as beautiful as the tower of David, built with
costly stones
Your breasts are standing like towers of zerubbabel

You are as bright as the sun and fair as the moon.
Who will not testify of these?
You are beautiful to behold Mkpurumma m
 You are pleasing to my eyes and captivating to my soul.

TELL THE WORLD

Tell the world we went to commune with our maker
Tell the world we went to fellowship with our brethren
Tell the world we went where we will find solace in this hard
time
But what did we get in return?
In a coffin we are now
We were sent to a journey of no return
As we lifted our hand and closed our eyes in prayers

Alas! a thunderous sound we heard
Like we all see in a movie
We heard the sound of gunshot
Like barracks of army in a war front they were shooting
In twinkle of an eye we were wiped out from the surface of the
earth
Like a carcass we lay,
In a pool of our own blood we laid helplessly

Where did we go wrong?
Who did we offend?
Our lives cut short and our dreams terminated
This time we came again, but now in a coffin
Unable to lift those holy hands
Lips firmly tight and eyes shut down forever.

I WILL FIND LOVE AGAIN

I will love again even when all ships are down
I will love again even when all hope are gone
I will love again even though my heart is broken
I will love again even if my love is gone
I will love again even if breakfast is served
I will love again even if there is no more reason to love
I will love again even if my first love betrayed me

I will love again even though I was used
I love again even though I have cried and told myself I will
never love again.
I will love again even when her words cuts deeper than that of a
knife
I love again even though there is a weight on my shoulder

Like the freedom field where horses run,
I will keep on chasing after it
Like a dog after a hare, I will keep running
A bottomless well,
 A flame, a ride
A wave of passion,
I believe I will find love again.

OH! MY SON

My heart is broken!
My blood is shattered!
My veins are beeping!
Tears has been my food all the day
Darkness beclouds my reasoning
I feel I could just tear myself apart
What storm that shook the ocean of my sleep
They have taken away the only thing that brings me happiness
Oh! My joy has been terminated
The birth of Nnamdi closed the mouth of the gainsayers
 And made those who call me barren bow their heads in shame
Now they have blinded the only eye which I see through
Of what use is life to me?
Those whole mongers wasted you,
 when you are about to reach the peak of your career
And when I was about to enjoy the fruits of my labor,
Oh! My heart is shattered
I wish I'm just dreaming
My heart has swelled with a sea of tears
May your killers have no rest nnamdi
Avenge your death oh! my son.

THE BEAUTY BEHIND THE SMILE

Her smile to me was like wine
Golden wine thy word of praise
She exnorates beauty from her crown
Her body is a wonderland
She sings like the voice of angel
Her voice is music to my ear and medicine to my soul
Her love is like that a mother Hen has for her chicks
Strength and dignity are her clothings

She smiles to erase memories
She smiles to ease pain
Behind the smile is a story untold
But she chooses not to let her past situation determine her
present condition
Her smile is contagious
She lifts up the room with her smile and never wants to leave
you the same without infecting you with it.

I IMAGINED IT

Life is a lighted window with a closed door
While in the mines of dark and silent night
I delve and find strange fantasies there
All my words are but crumbs that fall down from the feast of
the mind
Some days my thoughts are just like cocoons,
Hanging from dripping branches in the gray wood of my mind
I put them down in my heart as it is in my mind
I began to dream and hope that one day they will come to
reality

Everything I dreamed of seems difficult
Things were falling apart
I was laughed to scorn by foes I call friends
This can never come to reality!
This is a waste of time and energy!
It can only happen in your mind they say
The echo of their voices was still ringing like a bell in my ears
that very night
Could they be right? I began to think

Notwithstanding I paid deaf ears to their scorns
And developed the image of everything I wanted in my mind
If you can dream it, you can achieve it I told myself
Then I remembered the holy book says "as a man thinks in his
heart so is he"
I began to imagine it
With that My confidence level boosted
Even the least part of my dreams I imagined it
I went forth with hope and fear into the wintry forest of my life

Lo! and behold to my greatest surprise I saw them manifest
Yes! It happened
Before my very eye I watch them grow
Before my very eye I watch them advance
They grew till the room couldn't contain them any longer

I screamed but words weren't coming out of my mouth
The light flows into the bowl of the midnight sky
Tears of Joy ran down my cheek
Pains has ended, tears has stopped, doors has opened
I imagined this, now it is happening before my very eyes.

COULD SHE BE MINE?

The half Moon have appeared in the sky
But I couldn't see it, all I saw was her glamorous face
She dissipated the darkness of the hour
When I look into her eyes,
they were sparkling and glowing with her face,
Shining brighter than the sun
I can see her beauty even in darkness

I was dumbstruck fixing my gaze at this haunting beauty
The sparkle in her eyes were still there
The magnificent of it made me wonder if I she could ever be
mine
And what I would do if I were lucky enough
to shuttle up to stardom
My arms were akimbo as she held my thighs,
And Looked straight into my eyes

The rain was pattering on the roofing sheet,

as thunder grumbled in the sky
I thought about it as I gaze at her melanin skin
The tumult was punctuated with momentary blinding flashes of
lighting.

I WISH

So I sat spinning still, round this decaying form,
The fine threads of rare and subtle thought
I wished it was a dream but sadly it wasn't
I grew up in a decent home
A home where joy abounds and happiness never ceases therein
Modesty and decency was our watchword
Truth and honestly became our apparel
An example to others we were,
And we became the envy of many

I became a blind fool of fate and slave of circumstance,
And was deceived by folks I call friends
I forgot so quickly where I came from,
 And yielded to peer pressure and persuasion to make it quick

Evil communication they say corrupt good manners
I never understood this until a victim I became
Just a night with them I was apprehended
All escaped except me
Then it dawned on me that I was doomed
What will I tell my mum
I was the hope of my mum and my sibling's confidence

Oh! I wish I knew the end from the beginning
I wish I didn't yield to peer pressure

This I cried out in the courtroom
Before the judge made the pronouncement
I have been sentenced to life imprisonment
Oh! I am finished and doomed

I turned and saw my mum
Her eyes flowed rivers
She has cried her eyes out and tears were no longer coming
forth
The last word I heard from her before I was taken by the guard
was
Bring back, my son!! She wailed and fell on the floor

I was so ashamed of myself
Tell my mum I'm sorry
For the pains and embarrassment
Tell her to behold and watch over my other siblings
My heart swell with a sea of tears
The drums of time have rolled and ceased
I wish it was all a dream.

THE SCARS

In the land of the unknown
Full of nameless faces,
I once remember,
We were rejected by Our own
Shades were thrown to us for no just cause
We were called abominations

That we were a menace to the society
They said it's sacrilege for a womb to begat two flesh at once
We were despised are humiliated
Twins are accursed they echoed
It's an abomination and a sacrilege

Alas, we were banished from our fatherland
To land, we know not
Those who were meant to protect us have given us up to death
Scars were put on my sister's face
I was inflicted with sharp pain and it pierces my eyes
We screamed for help but helps seems far away from us
As my sister wailed in pain, I stood up
Alas, the worst has been done

My sight has been taken away
 As blood gushed like the rivers through my hands
Each blade of grass was a tiny bayonet pointed firmly at our
bare feet

Enough of the torture she screamed
Enough of the humiliation she cried out
We are humans for God's sake
Why do you treat us as if we are criminals
We didn't commit any crime
We are just two flesh that came out of one body
We are twins and is a gift from God,
Not an abomination

As we stood in reminiscent
We were nothing but those whose world is but the trembling of
a flare
Indeed scars are a roadmap to our Soul.

BEYOND LOVE

Laying on the shoulder of a giant
I was consumed by his love
The beauty of love, a joy forever
Joy unspeakable with waters and stars
Stars with storms of flour and a clash of lightening
Lightening that bonded the soul, spirit, and body
Two bodies subdued and became one

Kiss me with kisses on your lips
For your love is better than wine
Sing unto me the voice of an angel
For your voice is music to my ears and medicine to my soul
Shield me with your love
For strength and dignity are your clothing

Oh! Look up and see the birds
They waggle their rectrices at the sound of the melodious voice

The seas and oceans couldn't resist it when you sing as they
came and bow in worship
Thy song has been roses, soft and fragrant
With no thorns left in thy bosom
Every rose has its thorns
Just like every night has its dawn
I so longed for it as the deer pants for the water.

THE BEAUTY BLACK QUEEN

All shades of black
The beauty black queen
Her smile to me was like wine,
Golden wine thy word of praise
I will praise you for your body is magnificent,
Lithe as leopards limbs

She exonerates beauty from her crown
Her body is a wonderland
The African sand sprinkled on her melanin skin
Her song was an array of bright colors,
Swirling around the air

I will listen to you till dawn black queen,
For your voice is silky smooth,
And music to my ears
Oh! Look unto her glamorous face,
Do you see the lightning smile as it spears the night?
Her smiles lit up the room

When I was lost in the sea of nameless faces
Her words are chains of lead,
To remind me of how powerful I am.

PEACE

Gone are days
Days filled with sorrow
Sorrow turned tears
Tears that run through my nostrils like rivers
Rivers ever flowing
Flowing like living waters

Oh! I feel this peace
Peace of contentment
Contentment that bring happiness
Happiness that grants satisfaction
Satisfaction as a result of a fulfilled desire
Desires I longed for,
Is here ever before me like a dream

Now look into my heart and read through my mind
Mind that was filled with worries, now an utmost serenity I feel
therein
The tranquility that supersedes human understanding
The heartsease I crave for
The peace of mind I always desired
Is here to stay with me forever.

INNOCENCE

How pure is their heart
How unbiased is their mind
Their Innocence and honesty is second to none

Their prayers can move mountains
You want to get quick answers to your prayers
Tell a child to pray for you
Meek and lonely, gentle and mild
No wonder the holy book says,
Whosoever that will enter the kingdom will have the mind as
theirs.

They always tolerate, bearing no grudge with anyone
Have you been to where they play, you'll see selflessness in
action
Should I talk about their Innocence, is a story for another day.

A QUEEN AND MORE

Have you seen a queen without a crown
A goddess with a charm of love
Heart flowing like rivers of living water
 She conquers,
Got the mindset of a queen
And the heart of a warrior
Full of invisible scars
But never give up at all
What she survived may have killed many
She is the definition of a strong woman

She accepts her flaws
And ready to make it better
She loves fully, have no grip on pride
She stands for what she believes in

And endures every challenges that comes her way
She is Queen.

IF ONLY

Leaving a normal and care free life
Just like any other person
They call me an introvert
But I love me they way I am
 love my alone moment
For therein lies creative thought
Inspirations pours out like
Rivers of living water
I learnt how to abase and abound

Was skeptical in meeting him
Although I knew something was wrong
Cause my inner being never lies to me
 Using defense mechanism
Decided not to accept what the being spoke of
And Yielded to my emotions
In a twinkling of an eye
Just like we all see in a movie
The hedge was broken and
The laws of purity was defied
It happened as though I was unconscious

But it was a reality
It now dawned on me that all was infatuation

Oh! What have I done?
Should not have let my imagination control my emotions
Taught he loved me as he affirmed
But no, all was infatuation
Managed and staggered back home
It was like a nightmare,
wished I listened to that inner being

If tears can change anything
Only if I could turn back the hands of time
I wish I could
Wish could be my old introverted self
But it was a daydream
Alas did has been done

Weeks turn to months
Wasn't feeling myself
Alas! behold,
Found out I was with a child
How possible could this be?
I asked,
But the question sounds more
Like a rhetorical question
Became a single mum all of a sudden

 Lived like one who has no future
My Educational ambition was terminated
And the goals and dreams I often dream of

All is now a mere dream.

END BRUTALITY!

They said they are our friend,
But when you run to them when in danger,
They slaughter you like a ram,
We are tired of staying much hours on highway
All in the quest to meet your selfish demands,

A journey of 3 hrs is now 6hrs why?
Because of the selfishness of this terrorist in uniform,

Seeking for bribery and won't release you until you succumb to
their incessant demand,
There maliciousness is nothing to write home about,

Where have we gone wrong?
Is it a crime to be young and successful?
Why are you killing us?
Why are you trying to make the labors of our heroes past in
vain?
Is only a mad man that builds a house and destroys it with his
own hands.

Oh! our fathers land,
Life's have been wasted
And dreams shattered
Enough of the killings and bloodshed.

COULD THIS BE LOVE?

I tried to stop
But it keeps coming
In and out it flows like a river

The thoughts so genuine
Engrambled by imaginations
Should I stop thinking?
Should I let it roll away?
Should I let my imaginations control my emotions

It's sublime
It's ecstatic
Could this be love or something greater than it.

DADDY'S LOVE

With heavy sighs and tender smiles
With love in glistening eye
He looked deep into my eyes and saw the trembling in my soul
He brushed the hair out of my face
Touched the nape of my neck
And breathed gently into my neck
He said hey! Baby girl wake up
You're late for school.

SHAMELESS LOVE

In her lowest valley she was
In a deplorable state she lay
She was a mere fragment of what she had been
When he saw her, his head began to spin
The bitter taste of bile rose up in his mouth.
The ground seemed to slip beneath his feet
She was not dressed in the fine clothing he has given her

Her hair was in total disarray
Her nails were not manicured
She stood on the slave table in the marketplace
Her dress was torn, her hair tattarted
Her skin was smudged

Her naked knee were trembling
Her dirty face was wet with tears
The men were jeering and talking about her obscenely
But not for Jide, he was feeling around in his purse
He was willing to spend all that he had to buy her.

MY MOTHER'S HOUSE

I'm reminded of my mother
A gentle woman with the strength of a million males
To build a home and the power to create a family
I can easily recall my childhood days

The smell of biscuits, the sound of laughter
The touch of affection was everyday occurrences
Those were days when home was a reality not a myth
That is acted out more adeptly on television screen,
Than in the lives of those who watch
My mother belong to a day of grace that defiance finances

She was one not because of the abundance of class she
demonstrated,
I can still see the plain stretched dress,
That she ordered from a catalog
The tiny belted waist and the flowing skirt
Were draped by apron,
 As he seshayed through the house as if it was a castle
The floor creaking and the screen door was in need of repair

She still brought to the house an essence of femininity,
That transformed the tattered building,
Into a place that was rushed home to be
Be it ever so humble, it was still home
Home not because of its designs but because of its occupants.

My father bought the house but my mother transformed it to a home.

SWEET PAINFUL MEMORIES

Never have I imagined or thought
That this could happen
I thought what we shared was love
You shared everything with me
We were more than best friends and our love grew deeply

You were the shoulder I cry on when I'm down
 And my consolation when I'm in distress
You were my strength when my strength failed me,
You have no idea how my heart leaps
whenever I hear the sound of your voice
And how I stupidly smile whenever I hear you call me "Obim"
Why do you have to do this?

I knew something was wrong when there was a change in your
attitude
All of a sudden you started keeping secrets
And being too busy for me
Not doubt life is full of roses and thorns
Life often gives us what we want
It's so painful to see that what we once
cherished is no more
That the sweet river which once flowed is now stagnant

Not in my wildest imagination,
have I ever taught that this could happen
I feel like I'm going crazy
I feel like running mad
But it is what it is
It's been years but I still feel the pain.

THE SOUND OF MUSIC

We listen and enjoy the chirping of birds and the humming of
crickets
We turn on the music
But the music seems to distract us
From the weary road we travel
Music brings a certain sense of well being to us

Individual notes that are constructed for the production of
harmonious pitch
When the note are discordant, they sound like noise
When they are orchestrated into harmony,
They sound like tranquility of gentle souls
So is life, life is very much like music
But no orchestra can maintain harmony
Without the conductor to maintain time and structure

Your maker is the one that orchestrates the affairs
 That tend to create the noise of stress
Without him, life sounds like a junior high school band
warming up for march
He brings calmness and order to a chaotic world
So take a moment to inhale a deep breath of fresh air
And exhale every stress you have ingested
And turn the noise of your life into the music you want to hear.

LOVE IS TO LIFE

Love is to life what a scent is to a rose
It is the spice of life
It adorns life as clouds decorates the sky
From the cooing sound of a contented baby,
To the calm breathing of an aged grandmother
There is constant need for appreciation and affection

Love is the magic elixir of the soul
There is no drug that can compare with the passionate feeling
that are aflame when the heart is in love
It is love that cause the heart to pump honey to the soul
It is the sweet taste of honeycomb, that satisfy the taste bud of
the soul

Without love, life taste bland
What can compete with love
It has kept the sick man alive and man the well man feel sick
It is love that gives us courage and yet same love makes us
afraid
It weakens the mighty and strengthen the feeble

It can make an average person feel extraordinary
It has the ability to alter our perception and heighten our
vulnerability
It is that same love that made Christ to die
And that same love made him rise again.

CHILDHOOD MEMORIES

Surrounded by water
Immersed in my dreams
Admiring a flower
Crossing the midst

Collecting seashells
Wishing too deep
Protecting my world
Feeling misfit

Looking for rainbow
Loving too much
Missing my childhood
Counting stars.

BEFORE YOU LEAP, LOOK.

Life! this is what it is
Only if you can see it, but no
You have been blindfolded to what appeared before you
A misleading falsehood,
A willful perversion of facts
You may never get the view of the other side
The only side you get to see is the only side unveil to you
A beautiful garden with a lot of fresh fruit also have rotten fruit
therein only if you can see it

Look before you leap
Don't be so happy when the most beautiful part of it is being
shown to you
What appeared before you is what you see
You haven't seen it whole
You haven't seen it all
Just like as it is at the mirror
It is deliberate trickery intended to gain an advantage

Don't be so quick to judge
Understand the principles of times and season
Allow time to unveil the other part

Hey young lad, All glitters are not gold
Never be in a hurry
Never be in a haste
For what you see will be captivating
But therein lies deceit, fraudulence and
 dissimulation
Never conclude yet
Though the cover might be beautiful and tempting
They are wolves in sheep's clothing
Don't fall for it
Beware of deception.

WHO COULD HAVE BELIEVED?

Who could have believed?
That the baby cry that was once yearned to be heard
Is now the one weeping every night in pain in bed

Who could have believed?
That the voice which wakes me up every morning
Is now the voice that shock me to my bones and brings
trcmbling

Who could have believed?
That the first man who was there to guide and lead me through
path of life
Is the one that has threatened me with a knife

Who could have believed?
That the hands that carried me and nurtured me to sleep day
and night
Is the one that has taken sleep away from my eye like a bat

Who could have believed?
That the man who i ran to naked without shame
 Is the one that has taken away my innocence like a game

Who could have believed?
That the man whose loins I came forth
Is the same man forcing his rod in me to come forth

Who could have believed?
That the first man I ever played sand games with

Is the one toiling with my destiny and messing with my mental
health

Who could have believed?
 That the man I call father
Can tear my life apart and leave it in shatter

I was just but a child
But was born with a fate to the blind
I called you father
but you did not bother
Can I ever heal from this trauma?
Because my life now is just like drama
I really need a healer
One whose voice can set me free from this dilemma.

* 9 7 9 8 8 4 0 4 2 9 0 7 5 *